THE CANDIDATE
IN THE RYE

A Parody of
The Catcher in the Rye
STARRING
Donald J. Trump

by

JOHN MARQUANE

Chapter One

If you really want to hear about me running for president, the first thing you'll probably want to know is what country I was born in, and what my experience holding political office is like, and what my tax returns say, and all that Mitt Romney kind of crap, but I don't feel like talking about any of that, if you want to know the truth. And if I'm being honest—I'm the best at the truth. I really am.

Where I want to start telling is November 6th, two days before the presidential election, when I decided to leave the campaign trail for good. I don't know if you know this, but I was the goddamn nominee of the Republican Party. Very big deal. It was the final push to get people to vote, and I was supposed to be in Pennsylvania or some swing state like that. I don't swing both ways myself, but I guess the Constitution lets the states do what they want these days.

So it was two days before the election when I got up at some rally and spoke my mind about the Mexicans and Syrians and Clintons and whatever. Then, in a meeting, my running mate, old Pencey, he gave me all kinds of crap about how I wasn't supposed to offend people two days before an election. He was saying I flunked foreign policy and hadn't been applying myself out there. He thought he had all the answers, now that everyone wanted him on the top of the ticket and all. He even tried to make me promise to stop offending people when I first picked him—especially after the blondes at Fox News started saying the president should be presidential, which is what China wants you to think, if we're going there. So I guess it looked like I might even get the ax on Election Day. They give guys the ax quite frequently in America. It has very good labor laws, America. It really does.

What I told old Pencey was, if he was so sure he knew what he was doing, then he could run the campaign himself. He has one good debate, and suddenly he's acting like he knows what the country wants to hear. If I couldn't say whatever came into my mind about anything at any time, what was the point of becoming president, anyway?

So I walked out of the meeting and didn't look back. I skipped all the press conferences and about a thousand other media stints they'd set up for me. Instead I decided to get on the Trump Force One and head back home to New York. What I figured was, I would say goodbye to all the Americans I met over the last eighteen months. I love Americans, actually, even if sometimes they just give you this look. Like you're trying to make America a little too great or something.

But first I told the pilot to fly around in circles for a few hours—you could see half the country from up there. Half the country, they just love me. And that was just the deplorables. I knew *they* wanted me to become president, but sometimes, at one of my rallies, or a fundraising dinner, or in the middle of a tweet-storm, I kind of wondered: did I even want to be CEO of America?

It's funny, really. I don't even know what I was running for—I guess I just felt like it.

Chapter Two

One of the reasons I was flying to New York City was to get some advice from old Dr. Ben Carson. He's this professor guy I'd hired to teach at Trump U, even though we don't have students anymore. We call it the U because it's a fun nickname, and because it's illegal to call it a university.

We landed the jet and I took the helicopter, which I like to call the Trump Force Other One, over to midtown Manhattan. That's where Dr. Carson had an office, in the old Trump U department of neurosurgery. What a lot of people don't know about real estate is, it's all in your head.

Dr. Carson was in his old office. All the professors had one at Trump U, though sometimes they nicknamed them "closets." And they all had a college degree, or something like that.

Old Carson got a real kick out of teaching, even though he was almost in his seventies. I'm in my seventies, but it's a different kind of seventies.

I needed some advice, now that I'd left the campaign. I was dropping in those dirty polls with everyone again, even working-class white males now. When they're saying classy white guys are going for Crooked Hillary, that's how you know the whole thing's rigged. Many people were saying that, actually. I had it from very good sources, some really wonderful sources, that lots of things were rigged.

Take the Democratic National Convention, for example. They'd rigged it for Crooked Hillary to get the nomination, and now everyone talks about her "qualifications" and "years of experience in public office." I used to think women were beautiful, but I guess now they can be crooks too. I didn't say it, I'm just pointing it out.

I walked right into old Carson's office. He was sitting in one of those rolling office chairs. Lumbar support, very important. First step in the door, I knew it was a mistake. He was reading *The New Yorker* upside-down, or some other lousy liberal rag. I'm not too crazy about liberals, anyway. I actually used to be one, but that's a whole other story.

"I saw the DM you sent," I said. He'd sent me this secret little tweet saying he was sorry how the debates had been going and that I should stop by before the election, because I guess after that there was no going back. But by the time I finished talking, he was already asleep.

Old Carson did that sometimes, nodding off and all. Real absent-minded professor type. He's the only guy I ever met who could take a catnap in the middle of a sentence while talking on live TV. One time he was mumbling something about the 2nd Amendment when it happened, and I wish I was kidding, it took a gunshot to wake him up. Another time he said "Islamic," and then he yawned a little, and then he said, "terrorism." The voters, they ate that stuff up.

"Sit down, Donald," he whispered.

That was the other thing about old Carson. He was always whispering, so you always had to lean in to hear what he was saying. Sometimes you'd lean in just to find out those things he was mumbling weren't even words.

He started stroking his chin. You never saw anybody stroke their chin as much as old Carson did. Very intellectual, Ben Carson. Though sometimes with those intellectuals you don't know if they're stroking their chin because they're thinking or because they're hungry or something like that.

"Have you told your campaign you're not coming back?" he whispered.

"Not yet," I said.

"How do you think they'll feel about it?"

"They won't take it well," I said. "They really won't." It's funny, really, how spontaneous I can be. Just take a few days off the campaign trail in the week before an election. People like that about me. I'm seventy-two years old but I've never had a grey hair. I really haven't. If you saw my hair you'd understand why I come off as more youthful than I am. Full head of hair, really full.

"You still have a chance," old Carson whispered. "Take a moderate stance or two, compromise."

If there's one word I hate, it's compromise. A word for phonies if there ever was one.

Then old Carson leaned back in his chair, stroking his chin like he had something real good to say. I wanted to leave the room. I could feel a speech coming. I don't mind speeches so much, but the only ones I really trust are my own.

"What happened to you?" he whispered. He whispered it pretty dramatic, for him. "What happened at the debates?"

"All the online polls said I won the first debate. But there was something wrong with the mic that made everything I said sound poorly-informed and barely thought out."

"You lost the debate because you knew absolutely nothing. You probably couldn't have even explained what the pyramids in Egypt were built for."

I nodded, just to get out of there faster.

"And not a single mention of the Constitution," he whispered. That's something that just drives me nuts. When I get up there, tell everyone what I think and what I want to do in this country, and they say I don't know the Constitution. "I don't think you ever once looked at the Constitution, the whole campaign."

"Well, I sort of thought about it a couple of times," I said. I didn't want to tell him that there are more important things than the Constitution. He loved the Constitution, got a real rush out of it.

"You thought about it, huh?" he whispered. "You thought about it."

The odd thing is, though, my mind kind of wandered while he was whispering and all. I live in Manhattan, and I was wondering about the pond in Central Park, up near 60th Street. I was wondering, with all the illegals there, where they went in the winter. I wondered if some guy from the Immigration and Customs Enforcement came in a truck and took them away to a zoo or something. Or if they just flew away.

It's important in meetings, to be able to talk about one thing and think about another. What's clever is you can just nod, and the other person will think you're listening and start to feel all good about themselves. People usually think of me as a businessman, but really you could say I'm just a guy who makes other guys feel good.

"What are you going to do, Donald? The debates were a bust, the only women who like you are the ones directly related to you, and you're still in some trouble with your tax returns."

"I'm not having too much of a problem with my tax returns," I explained to him. "I didn't have any fines or anything. I just didn't disclose them, or something like that."

"Can I ask why not?"

"Why not? It's a funny story. It's a pretty long one too."

The last thing I wanted was to get lectured by him about it. He wouldn't have understood it. It wasn't his sort of thing at all. One of the biggest reasons I didn't release my tax returns was because I was surrounded by phonies. That's all. For example, I had this debate moderator, Anderson Cooper, the phoniest guy I ever laid eyes on. At that debate, for example, in St. Louis, he's got that terrific smile on, really a terrific smile, as if we're all friends there. Except if you start saying something about money and women. Then they look at you like you've done something wrong when all you've done is speak what's on your mind, and what happened to be on my mind at that point was money and women. That Anderson Cooper, though, he'll listen to you talk about how much you respect money and women, smiling and all, and then when you finish he'll ask if there isn't something a bit wrong about what you said. I can't put up with that stuff. It makes me nuts, it really makes me so nuts. Say a little thing about most Muslims supporting terrorism, and he gives you this look, just this look.

"Do you care at all about your chances on Tuesday?" old Carson whispered. "You'll have regrets. You'll wish you thought before you spoke, Donald. Maybe even got a little shuteye first, like me."

"I'm just speaking my mind," I said. "I'm a bit of a wild card, Doc. That's why they like me so much. It's what the American people want. I should know, anyway. I'm fantastically American. Maybe the most American."

"Sort of, Donald. Sort of."

He was using that tone that people use when they think they know something you don't. So I got up from that swivelly chair and stood on my feet. Everyone's always saying these terrible things about my hands, but what they don't know is, I've got really big feet. Only a very few people know that.

"Can I offer you a sandwich?" he asked. "Some coffee? Maybe one last olive branch to the African-American electorate?"

"Sorry, Doc, but I've got to head back to the jet. There's this hat I have to get. It's this red campaigning hat I like, with one of those very, very white fonts. This hat, it says it wants to Make America Great Again." I came up with the hat in a dream I had once when I was trying to find something to hide my hair. So I had couple million made. "But thanks for the advice."

We hugged. All that homosexual crap.

"Try not to insult anybody, Donald. Strong military, protection of civil liberties. Remember the Constitution. If you ever feel an insult coming on, just say 'I love the Constitution' instead. Just two more days, Donald. Stay on message."

I left the closet and was walking out of the office when he shouted something to me, but it was hard to hear. I think he shouted, "Don't insult the family of a military serviceman killed in action," which I'm sure he meant in a nice way, and it was terribly good advice, but in another way it reminded me of a really nice time I had a few months back.

Chapter Three

There aren't any runways for planes in Manhattan. It's sad. I could build one of course, but they'd never let me. I didn't feel like being low to the Earth in a car or on my feet just then, so I had to take the Trump Force Other One again. What I like about it is how it says "TRUMP" on the front. That way I know it's mine. Imagine walking into a helicopter parking lot and they all look the same and you don't know which one is yours. It would take hours to find it. But I've never had hours, is the thing.

Flying across town, I scrolled through the contacts on my phone. I'm usually not a big conversationalist, but for some reason I wanted to give someone a call. I couldn't come up with anyone though. My wife Melania was at some fundraising event for my campaign or charity or both. My daughter Ivanka was asleep, and it wasn't any fun talking to someone who was sleeping. I thought about calling into Meet the Press or Morning Joe or whatever Fox News show was on the air, but not even that was any fun anymore. They kept trying to ask me things like am I sorry. It gets old real fast, having to say, "Sorry for what?"

So here I was with no one to call. Me, the about-to-be president of the United damn States of America, or something crazy like that.

I realized I accidentally had given the pilot my regular address, just out of habit and all—I mean I completely forgot I was going to shack up in a hotel for a couple of days and not go home till the election was over. I have the best memory of all time, but that doesn't mean it's perfect. I didn't think of where I was going till we were halfway over Central Park.

I knocked on the seat in front of me, where the pilot sat. "Hey there," I said. I'm always friendly with the pilots. Very important, becoming friendly with your drivers and pilots.

"Can you turn this chopper around when you get a chance? I meant to tell you I didn't want to go to the Tower. The thing is, I don't want to stay at any hotels on the East Side where I might run into some acquaintances of mine. I'm traveling incognito." The problem with people now is everyone thinks they're my acquaintance.

"Then where to?"

"Well—take me to the Trump then," I said.

"The Hotel or the Palace or the Plaza or the Parc or the Park?"

"The Hotel of course." I wasn't trying to insult him. People always think it's an insult when I criticize them. "I love the Constitution," I said, just to be safe.

But he was one of those guys who likes to give you a bunch of crap when you ask for something. "A helicopter's not a car, Mr. Trump. It takes time to turn around."

"Alright," I said. Then I had a question. "You know the illegals wandering around the pond at the bottom of the park? Walking around, bathing in the non-Trump water when no one's looking and stuff. Do you know where they go, in the winter, what happens to them? Do you have any idea?" I realized it was only one chance in a million. Maybe a billion, trillion.

"Are you off your rocker, Mr Trump? What are you talking about, the illegals at the park?"

"I'd just been wondering about it." Nobody likes it when you wonder about things, especially not about illegals. People'd rather you just put it off your mind. I wished I was in my jet, where I could just turn on the TV.

We flew over Manhattan, and I watched it all through my window. It was hard to make out any illegals from that high up. You've always got to keep an eye out—lots of guilty people in that park. You never know where the Central Park Five might be, now that they let them out. But the chopper was stocked with some Trump Waters and some more red campaigning hats, and I put one on, just as some kind of entertainment for myself. I removed it before we landed though. I didn't want the paparazzi and all.

We got there eventually, on his schedule, not mine. I swear I could have gotten us there faster, just by using common sense. But I tried to play it nice. "How would you like a complimentary Trump Water for your efforts?"

"No can do, Mr. Trump," he said. "Those are for you only. Rules are rules." He was a hardworking pilot and I respected that. Terrific personality.

After we landed, I gave them a fake name at the check-in. I said, "One room for Mr. Drumpf." Drumpf is an old family name of mine I guess. Family is everything and all, but then a bunch of losers tried to make fun of me for that name, Drumpf. It's an immigrant name. That's what happens when you're an immigrant in this country. They laugh at you like Drumpf is funny or something. And then they get mad at you when you do the same exact thing to the next immigrant guy.

They gave me this very crummy room, with nothing to look out the window at except the other rooms. Normally I get the penthouse, but that's just how it goes when you're Mr. Drumpf. I didn't care much. I was too depressed to care whether I had a good view or not. I'm even pretty great at being depressed, to be honest. But it was still nice for all the towels to have my initials on them. Something about that "T" shape really catches the water when you're trying to dry off those places that are hard to get.

The bellboy that showed me to the room was this very old guy around sixty-five. When I look in the mirror, I see a guy who's 30 years old, fabulous blood pressure, terrific vitals. But this poor guy, he was even more depressing than the room was. He was one of those bald guys that comb all their hair over from the side to cover up the baldness. Just looking at him got me feeling pretty low, so I put my hat back on for kicks.

What I wanted to do was fire whoever hired this guy. The thing is, he wasn't pretty enough to be a server. Hell, he wasn't even a she. Hostesses, receptionists, secretaries, whatever you call those people who sit at the concierge desks—what they really need to be is attractive. People like to see good-looking people when they come in, is all. It's just good business.

I looked out the window. It's a shocker what goes on in

America these days. I saw one Middle Eastern couple, refugees maybe, whose window faced mine. The wife was breastfeeding an infant right in front of the father. Crazy things going on in America these days.

A few windows over, I saw through this window, the blinds open, this man and a woman, half-naked. Anyway, the man was on his knees, let's say pleasuring the woman, if you can call it that. Very disturbing trend, nowadays. Girls who want you to do a million things before you get right down to business. I'm not making this up, very perverted girls, today. I'd say it's one of the biggest reasons for the tremendous discontent in the country today. We have tremendous problems in the county, and at least half of them come from women expecting men to do things that are just plain unnatural. And I've seen this trend go on for a long time. I knew about this trend all the way back in the 80s, if you know what I mean.

I used to sleep with so many women, I didn't have time to sleep. I think Viagra is wonderful if you need it, if you have medical issues, if you've had surgery. I've just never needed it. Frankly, I wouldn't mind if there were an anti-Viagra, something with the opposite effect. I'm not bragging. I'm just lucky. I don't need it. If you need Viagra, you're probably with the wrong girl.

I was dating lots and lots of women back then. I was out four or five nights a week, usually with a different woman each time, and I was enjoying myself immensely. They were great years, but that was pre-AIDS. No matter when it is, you have to have a certain way about you, a stature. I see successful guys who just don't have the Look. And they are never going to go out with great women. The Look is important. I don't really like to talk about it because it sounds very conceited, but it matters.

But this stuff is pretty compelling to watch, though, in a certain way. I mean here's this guy, on his knees, pleasuring this woman. And he's this muscular, good-looking guy, and she's a seven, seven-and-a-half *max*. Very hard for a woman with a flat chest to be a ten, and this guy, I wouldn't say he has the Look, but he wasn't far from it either. Not that I was looking at him like that or any of that crap. I mean, take me—I'm a very conventional sexualist, after all. Very conventional, very American sexual habits. And I'm good—I'm *damn* good when I want to be, if you know what I mean, but I also don't always want to be. Sometimes I just want to sit back and enjoy. That's the problem with girls these days. They want you to contribute. If I'm being honest, I've actually never had a truly intimate sexual experience with a woman. I wonder why that is, but not too much. Sometimes I just wonder.

Scrolling through my phone, just staring at the contacts, I was thinking of calling up old Marla Maples. You weren't supposed to call ex-wives up late at night, but I had a plan. If her daughter picked up, I would tell her I was some sales guy, which wasn't exactly false. It would have been so easy to get out of that call, if I had to. Only I didn't do it, because I didn't really want to talk to Marla anyway.

After a while I sat down in a chair and drank a couple of Trump Waters. I'm not saying you can taste the difference, but you can definitely feel it. I was feeling pretty horny. I have to admit it. Then, all of a sudden, I got this idea. I knew just who to call. I looked through my contacts and found a number I'd gotten last summer. It was the number of this news anchor. I think we'd gotten along, and she liked how assertive I was. She moderated one of the debates or something, asked me about ten thousand questions, and I even answered a few of them. So I give her a call. Her name was Megyn Kelly, and she worked at Fox News, which isn't as foxy as it sounds. That's just a funny joke I came up with.

It rang. Maybe she was asleep. I called three times before anyone picked up.

"It's me," I said. "Long time no talk."

"Hello?" she said. I could tell it was Megyn. "The hell are you calling this late for? And who is this?"

"It's lonely sometimes, running for office. I have so many offices, but the thing with offices is you always need one more. I'm very glad you picked up the phone."

"But who *are* you?" she said.

"It's me, Donald. Remember, you said I should give you a call sometime? I distinctly remember that."

"Donald . . . I most certainly did not tell you to give me a call, anytime." She was real angry now, for some reason.

"I just wanted to say, I remember having a great time on your —"

"You called me a bimbo," she interrupted me, "and said that I had, and I quote, 'blood coming out of my whatever' during the first GOP debate."

I thought for a second. "I did?"

"Yes, Donald. I most certainly did not invite you to call me, and I can't imagine why you would possibly want to speak with me at this hour."

"Oh, I don't know," I said. "Sometimes I'm out, doing press conferences, meeting Americans, and I just want to talk to someone . . . *real*, you know? I thought we could chat for a bit."

"About what? I was sleeping, for God's sake."

"How are you, anyway?"

"I'm fine, Donald. I'm just fine. What's going on, you calling this late at night? Are you going through something?"

"Do you ever feel like . . . people don't want to see the real you? All day, during the campaign, I have these advisors coming up and telling me not to say that Crooked Hillary got schlonged by Obama and a million other things I can't remember. But you, I think you know the real me."

"You've said things about women that would suggest you are a shallow, callous, ignorant man."

At least she paid attention to what I'd said. Most of my advisors didn't seem to pay attention, they were so worried about me saying the wrong thing about John McCain. Like if he was such a hero, what was he doing getting captured and stuff like that? Talking about it all the time, like getting your plane shot down and captured is some real big accomplishment.

"So," I asked her, "what are you up to tomorrow?"

"Covering the campaign, which, by the way—shouldn't you be getting some rest?"

"I can do a press conference in my sleep," I said. "Some of my best tweets came when I was wasn't even awake."

"Regardless. You are a pig with deplorable politics."

I think she was referring to the time I called women pigs, trying to throw that back in my face. People got real worked up about that one, and how I called them dogs too. I'll admit that doesn't make any sense, looking back, calling women pigs and dogs. Pigs and dogs have nothing in common. Are they pigs, or are they dogs? Sometimes I wonder. Anyway, I love all the animals.

So I said to old Megyn, "What's your address? I'll come to you."

"Absolutely not, Donald. Never, ever, ever." I hate it when girls say something like that, repeat the same word two or three times as if you didn't hear it the first time. If I wasn't going to listen the first time, then I definitely wasn't going to listen the second.

"Maybe I could just come over for an interview. Exclusive. How would you like that?"

Then I heard a big click. She'd hung up. I really should have laid the charm on thicker. I can really be a terrific charmer when I want to be. She was acting all aloof, which is a thing women do sometimes.

Chapter Four

It was after midnight when Megyn hung up on me, which means Asian markets were just about to open up. Very strange customs, in the East. They like to open their stock markets in the middle of the night, just to throw you off. Who knows what kind of stuff they'll come up with next.

I thought of giving my daughter Ivanka a ring. It's nice to talk to someone who doesn't think you're what's wrong with democracy. But I didn't want to talk to her about all that campaign crap. And if her mother picked up, I'd be in big trouble. Big trouble.

I wish everyone could meet Ivanka. She's smart, brilliant, and has this terrific figure. Talk about business acumen, she's been negotiating me down from the day she was born. I've always said that if she wasn't my daughter maybe I'd be dating her. She's a model, in fact. She's done some modeling. I have to say, if I weren't her father—well, you know what I'm saying. That's a joke I make sometimes. Some people don't realize I have a terrific sense of humor.

I remember when Ivanka was very young—she's still young, mind you—we would go on these long walks in Atlantic City, through my hotels and casinos and all. She's 34 now, and still pretty much a little girl, but I've always enjoyed being a father very much. But I don't kid myself. Life is very fragile, and success doesn't change that. If anything, success makes it more fragile. Anything can change, without warning, and that's why I try not to take any of what's happened too seriously. The real excitement is playing the game. I don't spend a lot of time worrying about what I should have done differently, or what's going to happen next. If you ask me exactly what all the deals I made add up to in the end, I'm not sure I have a very good answer. Except that I've had a very good time making them.

Anyway, I didn't feel like sleeping much, so I figured I'd go to the hotel lounge.

The bar was pretty quiet. The tables were all taken, but the place is named after me and all, so they went through all kinds of hoops to get me one. There were girls there, but they were all in their thirties and forties. A little too old for me, if you know what I mean. Some waiter asked what I wanted to drink. I asked for a Trump Vodka.

"We don't have that, sir," the waiter said. "They don't make that anymore."

"What about Trump Rosé? I don't even drink alcohol, I'd just like to look at a bottle with my name on it."

"All out, sir. They sold too well."

Hell, okay. I could have told him that. "Give me another Trump Water then, I guess."

I sat there for a while drinking it. I also had a Trump Steak, which if I'm being honest is probably just about the best thing I ever had. Still, I felt like crap. After a few drinks the bartender was closing tabs and cleaning up. I got two more Trump Waters before he finished. The bill totalled about a hundred bucks, which I didn't mind. That's the thing about me. I'm not loose with my money, but I'm not stingy either. I talked to the bartender about renegotiating the debt, but he was some kind of loser you couldn't deal with.

Then, and I don't know why, I couldn't stop thinking about my first wife, Ivana. That's what really drives me up the wall. A girl, even if she's half crazy or she wants your money, if she's got a terrific body you're gonna fall for her.

We got together back in the 70s. We were the best-known couple in New York City, or something crazy like that. Ivana, you know, she's got this great face, great chest, but don't let that throw you off—believe it or not, she's got a great mind too. I was just getting started in real estate, and you won't believe the kind of lawsuits they threw at me. Accusing me of racism, discriminating against minorities. Crazy to think of that, when I love the minorities. But I'd seen Ivana around and all, and then one night we're at this party. And I'm not so big on parties, because there's just so much phony conversation. Lousy guys who don't want to talk about the real issues we're facing—the Chinese, for example. Very big problem, the Chinese. Anyway, I'm having some lousy conversation about gender equality when I spot Ivana across the room. I'm a charismatic guy when I want to be, so I went on over to her.

Straight away, Ivana and I became real intimate. We'd go to Trump Golf Links in the Bronx. They call it that because it was my idea to construct a big grassy area for people to play golf on. Now, she was an incredible skier, almost made it to the Olympics in fact, but there's something about women and golf, if you know what I mean. They can be physically good, very good. But they don't have that instinct to win, which is probably one of my best qualities. My best quality is my temperament, though. I have an incredible temperament.

There was this one time, I remember, a Saturday night when Ivana and I stayed home to do our taxes. It was raining out, and we were having a miserable time, a really terrible time. IRS audits and all that crap. We were working it out together, and Ivana, Ivana's got a really good mind for this tax stuff. Very sharp. It was late, and we were nowhere close to being done, and you know what she does? She takes my hand, holds it. And she says to me, "What's it like to be The Donald?" She was the first one to call me that, The Donald. Can't forget something like that, even if you want to. When a girl calls you something like that, it pretty much changes your life.

Anyway, the bar had really cleared out. It's funny—whenever I'm out doing campaign events, all I feel like is being alone. But as soon as I'm alone, I wish there were people around. I wonder why that is.

I wanted to go somewhere people might recognize me, say a nice thing or two every now and then. So I called up my personal driver and had him pick me up. Told him to take me to Trump Model Management. At least someone there would be nice to me and all. I certainly like to feel good about feeling good sometimes, believe me.

The car I had was a real old one that smelled like the 70s,

like leather and perfume and winning. But there was almost nobody out on the street to see it driving along.

I kept wishing I could go home and stay up chatting for a while with old Ivanka. But finally, after I was riding a while, the driver and I sort of struck up a conversation. His name was Chauffeur. Probably from one of those fancy French families that lost the wrong war, and next thing you know, their descendants are driving me around.

The thing about employees is, you have to have them. I'm more than their boss, in a way. I enjoy it when they call me their patriarch, I really do. They don't have to worry about Obamacare, my people. I treat them really good with healthcare. It's a very important thing. The female employees are always causing trouble though. Pregnancy is a wonderful thing for a woman, it's a wonderful thing for a husband, but it's certainly an inconvenience for business. Whether people want to say that or not, the fact is that it's true. Sometimes I'd listen in on my employees' calls with a switchboard in my bedroom. I never really used it, but it was nice to know it was there.

Anyway, I thought maybe my driver might know about the illegals. "Hey, Chauffeur," I said. "You ever pass by the lagoon in Central Park?"

"The what?"

"The lagoon. That little lake thing. Where the illegals are. You know."

"Yeah, what about it?"

"Well, you know the illegals that swim around in it? In the springtime and all? Do you happen to know where they go in the winter, by any chance?"

"Where who goes?"

"The illegals. Do you know, by any chance? I mean does

somebody come around in a truck or something and take them away, or do they flee by themselves—go south or something?"

Old Chauffeur turned all the way around and looked at me. He was a very impatient-type guy. He wasn't a bad guy, though. "How the hell should I know?" he said. "How the hell should I know a stupid thing like that?"

"Well, don't get mad about it," I said. He was mad about it or something.

"Who's mad? Nobody's mad."

I stopped having a conversation with him, if he was going to get so damn touchy about it. But he started it up again himself. He turned all the way around once more. "The pretzel vendors don't go no place. They stay right where they are, the pretzel vendors. Right by the goddamn lake."

"The pretzel vendors, that's different. The pretzel vendors is different. I'm talking about the illegals," I said. "It's different for the pretzel vendors, the winter and all, than it is for the illegals, for Christ's sake. Use your head." I didn't say anything for about a minute. Then I said, "All right. What do they do, when the Immigration and Customs Enforcement comes? The ICE. Where do they go when the ICE comes?"

Old Chauffeur turned around again. "What the hell do you mean what do they do?" he yelled at me. "They stay right where they are."

"They can't just ignore the ICE. They can't just ignore it."

"Who's ignoring it? Nobody's ignoring it!" Chauffeur said. He got so damn excited and all, I was afraid he was going to drive the car right into a lamppost or something.

"They're terrified of the goddamn ICE. It's their nature, for Christ's sake."

"Yeah? What do they do, then? I mean if the stuff is frozen

solid, they can't wander around with their food carts and all."

"Are you talking about the pretzel vendors or the illegals?"

He didn't answer me, though.

I changed the subject. He was such a touchy guy. "Would you care to stop off and look at some models with me?" I said.

"I ain't got no time for no models, bud," he said. "Someone's got to wait outside in a car for you. How the hell old are you, anyways? Why aren't you home in bed?"

"I'm not a big sleeper," I said. "I like three hours, four hours, I toss, I turn, I beep-de-beep, I want to find out what's going on." Beep-de-beep is a funny little way I refer to checking the cyber.

When I got out in front of Trump Model Management, old Chauffeur brought up the pretzel vendors again. He certainly had it on his mind. "Listen," he said. "If you were a pretzel vendor, God would take care of you, wouldn't he? Right? You think the pretzel vendors all die in the winter?"

"No, but—"

"You're goddamn right they don't, Chauffeur said. "Maybe it's the same with the illegals then. But instead of God, it's Lady Liberty."

"But they're bringing drugs," I said. "They're bringing crime, they're rapists."

He just shrugged a little. "Whatever you say, boss."

He was about the grouchiest guy I ever met. Everything you said made him mad.

I headed up to the 5th floor on Spring Street, where they pick the models. It's pretty easy to be a Trump model. All you have to do is be a girl, at least 14 years old, between 5'8" and 6'0", gorgeous, and willing to work for free.

The security guard who let me in looked pretty confused.

All the security guards at Trump Model Management are also models. They get confused sometimes, but so do the bad guys when they try to break in.

"Mr. Trump?" the security lady said.

"Where is everybody?"

"It's three in the morning."

"Does nobody work around here?"

"Not really, at three in the morning."

"So now you're going to knock me for being here at three in the morning?" I said. "At least you know I'll be up, ready to take the call."

"The call? What call?" she asked. She didn't know anything about how running for president works.

"The call that comes at three in the morning when you're president. When the Chinese happen. I'll be there to take it."

"At a modeling agency?"

"At least I'll be somewhere, won't I? Won't I?"

"Yes, Mr. Trump. You'll definitely be somewhere."

She was a phony, alright. I didn't even bother saying good-bye. I just walked out and went down, down, down, all the way down to Chauffeur outside. Back in the hotel, I took a little nap. Not because I had to—just because I could.

Chapter Five

I didn't sleep too long—I don't need to sleep.

What I did do, I gave old Melania Knauss a ring. She's Melania Trump now, of course. I have a habit of putting my name on things. Whatever her name is, she's definitely old. She was already 46.

She's from Slovenia, which is different from Slovakia. I knew she was home because I told her to be. I wasn't too crazy about her, but I'd known her for years. She knew a whole bunch of plays and literature and smart stuff like that, but the problem was they were all in Slovenian. There's a reason you can't name any Slovenian plays, and it's not because of Crooked Hillary's import tax, I can tell you that. All I can tell you is they definitely have a word for "sex" in Slovenian. But I've never exactly asked.

When I called her up, first the maid answered. Then her father. Then she got on.

"How are you?" I asked. "I mean, how's life?"

"Fine," she said. "I mean—you know."

"Terrific. Well, listen. I was wondering if you wanted to go to a matinee today. Get out, see some culture or whatever. I'll buy the tickets like usual."

"Whatever you want, my Donald."

For a second, I was tempted to tell her to forget about the matinee. But we chatted for a while. That is, she chatted. I hate small talk. There's nothing huge about it. But she wasn't always so bad, no matter what the papers said about her plagiarizing and not being legal. It really doesn't matter what the media writes so long as you've got a young and beautiful piece of ass.

I told her to meet me under the clock at the theatre at two o'clock, and not to be late, because the show started at two-thirty. She was always late. Girls take forever to put on the makeup and face stuff, and I made the mistake of letting her have a whole makeup line. Melania Luxe Night, caviar-flavored. You wouldn't believe the stuff girls put on their faces these days. She gave me a pain in the ass, but she was really very attractive.

Then I went down in the elevator and checked out. I took out my wallet and sort of counted my money. I hadn't carried cash in ten, maybe forty years. I don't remember exactly what I had left, but it was no fortune or anything. I'm a goddamn spendthrift at heart. What I don't spend, I lose. Buildings, bankruptcies, bullion, you never know where it goes. You'd be surprised how a billion dollars can disappear.

It used to drive my father crazy how I spent money. You can't blame him. My father was quite wealthy, though. I don't know how much he made—he's never discussed that stuff with me—but I imagine quite a lot. One time he gave me a small loan of fourteen million dollars, and now I'm really rich.

I was getting hungry, so I went into this little sandwich bar called McDonald's for some breakfast. The good thing about fast food is at least you know what's in it. I had quite a large breakfast, for me—orange juice, bacon and eggs, toast and coffee, burger and fries, shake and soda, nuggets and McFlurry, and a side salad for the nutrients. Usually I just drink some orange juice. I'm a very light eater. I really am. That's why I'm so damn skinny, and that's without even trying. I got a lot of exercise from waving my arms at all the rallies. I probably burned a hundred calories just imitating that crippled guy that one time. My advisors said I should do that less, but really it'd be healthier if I did it more, if you think about it.

And my doctor, he said I'd be the healthiest individual ever elected to the presidency. Right on national TV. I'm not an expert, but he's probably right. You don't get to be a doctor for nothing in this country. It's funny—running for president, you don't even need any credentials. All my credentials are in my head. You wouldn't believe what's up there. I think so fast, it's crazy. There's no time to write any of it down. And besides, the only thing worse than doing paperwork is releasing it.

Once my stomach was full of food I could trust, I started walking over toward Broadway, just for the hell of it, because I hadn't walked somewhere in years. Besides, I wanted to find a record store. There was this record I wanted to get for Ivanka, called "Over There." It was a very hard record to get. It was about these little girls who wanted America to be great again.

I heard it at one of my rallies. "Enemies of freedom/Face the music/Come on, boys—take 'em down!/President Donald Trump knows how/To make America great/Deal from strength or get crushed every time." It really was a pretty song. I don't know how they did it, but they got me where it hurts.

I was lucky. The first record store I went into had a copy of "Over There." They didn't have a disk of it, but one of the clerks had a computer, and the computer had the cyber, and the cyber had a copy of it. They put it on a little black stick thing. They charged me five hundred thousand for it, because it was so hard to get, but I didn't care. I negotiated them down from seven-fifty. I'm the best negotiator. They didn't know it, but they were morons—I'd have paid a million for the thing. The crazy part is, the stick came on a little keychain, and they threw in the keychain for free.

Boy, it made me so happy all of a sudden. Deals are my art form. Other people paint beautifully on canvas or write wonderful poetry. I like making deals, preferably big deals. That's how I get my kicks.

I still had to get those damn theater tickets, so I bought a paper and looked up to see what shows were playing. I went over and bought two orchestra seats for "Hamilton." It was a benefit performance or something. I didn't much want to see it, but I knew old Melania would start drooling all over the place when I told her I had tickets for that, because Hamilton was on the ten dollar bill and all. Melania loves money. I mean, I do too. For all I know, that's why I love Melania.

I got the tickets for two grand off a scalper who didn't know what was best for him. He thought it was a lot, but it's nothing if you just paid half a million for the cyber stick. Einstein once said everything was relative. He's one of the few science guys who got it right. These days all the science guys are trying to shove their science down your throat. Then they get all mad when you don't fall for it. The concept of global warming was created by and for the Chinese in order to make U.S. manufacturing non-competitive. Things are never what they seem anymore. The temperature—it goes up and it goes down. I believe there's weather, I'll tell you that.

I was way early when I got there, so I just sat down on one of those leather couches. Finally, old Melania started coming up the stairs. She looked terrific. The funny part is, the minute I saw her I thought maybe we shouldn't divorce. I'm crazy. I didn't even like her much, and yet all of a sudden I felt like I was in love with her and wanted to stay married to her. I swear to God I'm crazy. I admit it. And that ring on her finger—brilliant gem, facets like you wouldn't believe. She really was worth marrying. All the hot ones are. Beauty and elegance, whether in a woman, a building, or a work of art, is not just superficial or something pretty to see.

"My Donald!" she said. "It's so nice to see you! It's been weeks."

She had one of these very embarrassing Slovenian voices. She got away with it because she was so damn good-looking, but it always gave me a pain in the ass.

"It's good to see you," I said. I meant it, too. "How are you, anyway?"

"Never been better, dear. Am I late?"

I told her no, but she was around ten minutes late, as a matter of fact. Time is money, as they say, and ten minutes is about three million dollars.

"I'm excited for the show," she said. I heard they have a nice diverse cast."

Diversity. If there's one word I never understood, it's diversity. I actually don't know what it means. Then, just to show her how crazy I am, I told her I supported diversity in melting pots, crackpots, all kinds of pots.

"Oh, my Donald, I always knew you did," she said. Then, right in the same damn breath, she said, "Promise me you'll let your hair grow longer. You've got such nice hair."

The show wasn't as bad as some I've seen. It was on the crappy side, though. It was about five hundred thousand years in the life of this one Mexican guy named Hamilton. Turns out it had nothing to do with the guy on the money. Talk about false advertising. I'd have never let this crap into Trump Magazine.

In the show, Hamilton's this illegal who goes to war and then everybody runs around and does that rap-singing thing the blacks do. I guess the Mexicans do it now too. They've got to be careful what habits they're picking up. Like I said back when I ran casinos, laziness is a trait in blacks. It's really a shame. A well-educated black has a tremendous advantage over a well-educated white in terms of the job market. I think sometimes a black may think they don't have an advantage or this and that. If I were starting off today, I would love to be a well-educated black. I've always had a great relationship with the blacks, but it helps that they love me too.

Old Melania didn't talk much, except to compliment the immigrants, because she was busy being politically correct and all, and because she was an immigrant or whatever. Then all of a sudden, she saw some jerk she knew on the other side of the theatre. Some guy in one of those very dark gray flannel suits, strictly Ivy League. Big deal. I went to an Ivy League school myself, but it was the best school in the country, so that's a different story. Ask around and anyone will tell you I'm really smart.

He was standing next to the wall, smoking himself to death and looking bored as hell. Old Melania kept saying, "I know that boy from somewhere." She always knew somebody, any place you took her, or thought she did. She kept saying that till I got bored as hell, and I said to her, "Why don't you go on over and give him a big old kiss, if you like staring at him so much?" She got mad when I said that. Finally, though, the jerk noticed her and came over and said hello. Then I realized who it was, speaking of immigrants. Old Barack Obama. Everybody's favorite non-Kenyan. Of course he would like this sort of play.

I got us out of there as fast as I could, before the damn thing even ended. It was Broadway though. The ending's always the same. Hamilton lives happily ever after, dances off into the sunset, and then they expect you to applaud. It's the same old story every time.

I was all set to take her home and all—I really was—but she said, "Let's do something crazy!" She was always having a crazy idea. The mind of a Slovenian can be very strange. "Listen," she said. "Do you have to be home any special time?"

"Me? No. No special time," I said. "Why?"

"Let's go ice-skating at Wollman Rink."

Now that was an awful low thing of her to do, and she knew it. The Wollman Rink was a real sore spot for me. Not a lot of people know its real name, or that I actually took over renovations when the city went over budget about a hundred years ago. I offered to save it and pay for the trouble myself. I did a terrific job really, under budget, no payment to contractors, ahead of schedule. I was proud of that rink, I really was. But then the city wouldn't let me change the name. Trump Rink—

great name, would have had that old Trump ring to it. They let me put Trump signs up everywhere and all, but no Trump Rink. It even says Trump on the website too. Take a look if you don't believe me.

My organization—Trump—still runs it. The thing that gets me about it is that it doesn't make any sense for it to be called Wollman Rink when it's a Trump rink. Wollman Rink is just another phony name.

"We can get some nice pictures taken," old Melania said. "A Kardashian did it last week." That's why she was so hot to go. She wanted to see herself on the front page with me one last time.

So we went, of course. She really did look damn good, though. I have to admit it. And don't think she didn't know it. She kept skating ahead of me, so that I'd see how cute her little ass looked. It did look pretty cute, too. I have to admit it. I'm automatically attracted to beautiful women—I just start kissing them. It's like a magnet. Just kiss, I don't even wait. And when you're a star, they let you do it. If you're me, you can do anything, really. But sometimes, a beautiful woman, she'll get these big phony tits. She'll change her whole look. And it's just not the same.

The funny part was, though, we were the worst skaters on the whole goddamn rink. I mean the worst. I'm the most athletic, but it's different on skates. The ground doesn't play by the same rules. The whole game's rigged, I can tell you that much.

"Do you want to get a table inside and have a drink or something?" I said to her finally.

"That's the most marvelous idea you've had all day," she said, like it was true or something.

The waiter came up, and I ordered a Coke for her. I said it before, but I've never seen a thin person drinking a Diet Coke. Just an observation. I tweeted that once and it did just amazing. Sometimes I wonder why some of my tweets do better than others. I guess sometimes you win a little and sometimes you win a lot. I'm a winner—I have a lot of money, everybody loves me. People don't get that I'm a winner. I like thinking big. If you're going to be thinking, you might as well think big.

Just thinking about it kind of got me in a mood.

"Hey, Melania," I said.

"What?" she said.

"Do you ever get fed up? I mean do you ever get scared that everything is going to go lousy unless you do something? I mean do you like America, and all that stuff?"

"It's a terrific bore."

"I mean do you hate it? I know it's a terrific bore, but do you hate it, is what I mean."

"Well, I don't exactly hate it. You always have a—"

"Well, I hate it. Boy, do I hate it," I said. "I hate that I can't land my helicopter on top of any building I want. I hate that if I want a good old-fashioned taco bowl, I can't get it from a good old-fashioned American, like taco bowls were copyrighted by Mexicans or something. And I hate traffic lights. What do we even need a red light for? Shouldn't we always be going forward?"

"Don't shout, please," old Melania said.

"Take cars," I said. I said it in this very quiet voice. "Take most people, they're crazy about cars. I'd rather have a goddamn helicopter. A helicopter is at least above everyone else. In a helicopter you can see America for what it—"

"I don't know what you're even talking about," old Melania

said. You could tell she wanted me to change the damn subject.

Then, all of a sudden, I got this idea. "Look," I said. "Here's my idea. How would you like to get the hell out of here? Here's my idea. I know this guy down in Jersey and we can borrow his yacht for a couple of weeks. He used to go to the same school I did and he still owes me about a million bucks, or I owe him, or something like that. What we could do is, tomorrow morning we could sail up to international waters, and all around there, see. It's beautiful as hell up there, It really is. I could go back into real estate, buy up some of that space. Hell, if global warming's real, all that water's going to be land soon or something. And if it is, we'll just make the whole Atlantic into one big island. And we'll put a casino on it. I could be the President of International Waters. And you could be the First Lady of International Waters. Honest to God, we could have such a nice time. Doesn't that sound nice? Come on. Would do you say? Will you do it with me? Please."

"You can't just do something like that," old Melania said. She sounded grouchy as hell. Like it was that time of the month or some crazy thing like that. She knows I don't like to think about those womanly things.

"Why not? Why the hell not?"

"Stop screaming at me, please," she said. Which was crap, because I wasn't even screaming at her.

"Why can't we? Why not?"

"Because you can't, that's all. Because the election's tomorrow."

"What's the matter? Don't you want to go? Say so, if you don't."

"Mogoče pa ne! Mogoče vam niti ne," old Melania said. Starting up with the Slovenian crap again.

We were both pretty grouchy by then. You could see there wasn't any sense trying to have an intelligent conversation. I should have known, with her being politically correct and all.

"Come on, let's get outa here," I said. "Sometimes I wish I were back with Ivana, if you want to know the truth."

Boy, did she flip when I said that. I know I shouldn't've said it, even if there isn't anything I've ever said that I'd take back. But she was depressing the hell out of me. Usually I never say crude things like that to girls. Boy, did she hit the ceiling. She was acting like it was made of glass or something.

Chapter Six

I didn't want to spend any more time with Melania, but as soon as I was alone, I wanted to talk to someone again. So I went back to Ivanka's apartment at Trump Tower and snuck into her room. I don't think she was too happy about it, but it's my name on the building, not hers.

"How's the conversion going?" I asked her. That's something I always ask her. See, she married this guy who's Jewish. She read the Torah and all that crap and now she's a Jew. It's not a bad thing—I'm actually very popular with the Jews. Very popular. I always knew Israel would be just fine if I got elected.

"Mom will be furious if she finds you here," Ivanka told me. Her mother and I divorced when Ivanka was nine years old.

Even Ivanka really gets under my skin now and then, just like her mom, Ivana. Sometimes you add a "k" to a name and it doesn't make any difference.

"You need to go on TV and tell America how to be great," she said. "Just don't say anything offensive this time. Why do you do this to yourself? All you have to do is stay on message. Please. Please." It depressed the hell out of me that even Ivanka was saying this.

"I've got enough campaign managers already," I said. "And this has been just about the worst presidential campaign I've ever been on. Full of people telling me what I can and can't say. Like when I'm talking about building a wall with Mexico, and I go to Mexico to tell them about it. Suddenly everyone's saying all kinds of stuff about me being a racist. Race has got nothing to do with it. Mexicans aren't even a race, and if they were, I would be very popular with them. And don't even get me started on Crooked Hillary. She's the one who founded ISIS, after all, and all that Islamic terrorism crap. All I do is talk about her physical appearance twenty times and everyone's saying I'm a sexist about it. Do people not want an attractive president?"

Then Ivanka gave me this look, just this look. Like disappointment. And that just kills me, it really does. It really does make me depressed. Like she thinks I should've just kept my mouth shut and stayed on message.

"You'd think at least the other Republicans would be nice about it," I said, "but they're just lousy cheaters like everyone else. I did like this one guy, Ronald Reagan. He's dead, but he's always been a real inspiration to me. Now there's a guy who had more important qualifications than being a politician. Acting isn't that different from being president, if you think about it.

You just go on TV and say some words and the audience cheers, but you don't really have to know anything."

"I know, Dad," she said.

"And this Mexico thing, it's really just a lousy helluva thing. Makes me real depressed sometimes. Did you know there's about eleven or twelve million Mexicans living in America that never came here legally?"

"Dad. I know."

"And I have this plan for a wall and all. A wall all along the border with Mexico. So what I do is I go to Mexico and tell Peña Nieto, the President of Mexico and now a good friend, about this whole wall idea and how Mexico is going to pay for it."

"Please, dad."

"And all I want, as I've said about ten thousand times, is to make America great again, and suddenly the media's saying all these terrible things about me. It really depresses the hell out of me. I don't think there's anything racist about not wanting Mexicans in our country."

"Dad. Just—" She shook her head. "I can't even."

She was staring at me now. She just has one of those stares, like she's seeing something you don't, because the problem with being a person is that you can't see yourself and all when you're busy being you.

"You think everyone's against you," she finally said. And that just made me feel terrible. Just terrible.

"I don't think everyone's against me. Just the Democrats, and the Republicans. Most of the Republicans, and all the Independents."

"Name one person you think isn't lousy or a phony. One person that you think is on your side."

"There's loads of people on my side. I'm very popular."

"Okay. Name one."

"Someone I really trust?"

She nodded, and that just made me feel more depressed.

"There's not a single person you think's on your side, is there?"

"Oh, there's millions. Millions. Have you seen the polls?"

"I'm not talking about polls. Who do you trust?"

Of course I didn't know the answer, if she really wanted the truth. "What about you? I trust you."

"Besides me," Ivanka said. "Your daughter doesn't count."

"Of course you count. You count. I've always said if you weren't my daughter, maybe—maybe we could date. Isn't that funny?" I can be very funny sometimes.

"Do you even want to be president, Dad? Do you even really want to make America great again? Or do you just want to make *you* great again? You should have stuck to real estate. Casinos. Steaks. Literally anything else."

"Don't you see?" I said. Ivanka, she didn't understand. "Life's about more than casinos and steaks. Life's about making all those casinos and steaks mean something."

"Then you should have prepared for the debates," she said. "You should have known the difference between Hamas and Hezbollah. You should have known not to play footsies with Putin. You want to win, but you do everything off the cuff."

"It never matters what I really want, out on the campaign trail. Nobody wants to hear anything. If I could just leave all this behind, not feel an obligation to make America goddamn great again."

"Then tell me what it is you want," she said.

"You know that novel, *The Candidate in the Rye*?"

"It's *The Catcher in the Rye*. It's by J. D. Salinger."

Ivanka really knew her stuff. Big reader. I never had the time to read, myself. It turned out she wasn't wrong. I always thought it was *The Candidate in the Rye*. There were a lot of things I didn't know, back then.

"Are you sure it's not the *candidate*?" I said. "I've never read it, but I've always imagined this huge open plain, along the southern border. Huge and all desert-like, without mountains or hills or anything. And I'm standing on the border, just on our side of this huge river they call the Rio Grande, which I'm pretty sure in English translates to the big thing of Rye that Salinger's talking about. It's my job to find all the Mexicans coming across the border if they start to swim across, or go through one of those tunnels. And if I don't catch them all, send them back, something terrible might happen. I would spend my whole life doing it. No campaign, no Oval Office. Just me out there, saving all the Mexicans from themselves. I don't know. Maybe it sounds corny. But that's all I ever wanted."

And then Ivanka did something that really killed me. I thought she was a little mad at me, about saying whatever showed up in my mind and all. But now I could tell she was just sad. She reached out and squeezed my hand. It damn near killed me, I swear, it was so nice.

"Tomorrow's Election Day, Dad. They're gonna gut you out there unless you set things right. Get on TV, and just stay on message." She looked worried about me. My own daughter, and she was worrying about *me*.

"Then what am I supposed to do?" I said. "Tell me what you want me to do and I'll do it, if that's what you really want."

"Alright," she said. "Today, and tomorrow, please, please, please just don't say anything about minorities, or veterans, or women. Don't say anything about the police, or the military, or beauty pageant contestants, or the press, or the media, or your ex-wives, or how much money you have, or how paying no taxes makes you smart, or about Islam, or Muslims, or Syria, or Lebanon, or Iraq, or Afghanistan, or Iran, or Mexico, please nothing about Mexico, or about John McCain, or Megyn Kelly, or Hillary Clinton, or Bill Clinton's affairs, or Gennifer Flowers, or menstruation, or sex, or bodies, nothing about bodies, living or dead, or about Jill Stein's face, or Hillary Clinton's face, or Rosie O'Donnell's face, or Trump University, or Obama's birth certificate, or Benghazi, or ISIS, or Bernie Sanders, or Elizabeth Warren, or Jeb Bush, or The New York Times, or Bill de Blasio, or NAFTA, or the TPP, or the cyber, or Carly Fiorina, or Ted Cruz, or Marco Rubio, or the Khans, or Crimea, or Putin, or Russia, or me, or anyone, anyplace, or really anything at all. Or you."

We were quiet for a while.

Then I said to Ivanka, "I don't care what a damn bunch of phonies think." And I stood up, because I couldn't stand to sit there. I really couldn't stand it one more second, I swear.

What I wanted to do, I wanted to phone up this guy who was my advisor at the campaign, Roger Ailes. He lived a couple hours upstate. He quit Fox News. Or they quit him. But that's different from getting fired. So he took this job teaching me how to be a politician. He tutored all the greats—Nixon, Reagan, I think that's it.

"I have to make a phone call," I said. "I've got to go."

While I was walking toward the door, old Ivanka said, "Dad!" and I turned around. She was standing there in a gold dress I got her. She looked so pretty. "It's not over till it's over."

Yogi Berra said that once. And now so had she.

Then, all of a sudden, I started to cry. I couldn't help it. It scared the hell out of old Ivanka when I started doing it, and she came over and tried to make me stop, but once you get started, you can't just stop on a goddamn dime. I thought I was going to choke to death or something. Finally I stopped. But it certainly took me a long, long time.

Then I finished buttoning my coat and all. She told me I could sleep with her if I wanted to, but I said no, that I'd better beat it, that I had to go see Roger Ailes and all.

Then I took my red campaigning hat out of my coat pocket and gave it to her. She likes those kind of crazy hats. She didn't want to take it, but I made her. I'll bet she slept with it on. She really likes those kind of hats.

Chapter Seven

Roger Ailes has this real modest place a couple hours upstate, just a nine-thousand square-foot kind of place. I'd been a few times when Ailes invited me hunting, and it's really quite a nice place. I called up the Trump Force Other One and decided to head over there. What the hell else was I supposed to do?

The thing about Roger Ailes is that he's a real deep thinker. Real profound guy. You watch the news, there's all this crap about how he tells all these women how beautiful they are, like it's a bad thing, like people don't want to feel beautiful. That kinda stuff really bugs the crap out of me sometimes.

He met me at the landing pad and we shook hands. We both have a real strong handshake. Boy, was it nice to see a friendly face.

"Come have a drink with me," Ailes said. The place was a mess. Boxes full of buffalo wings and pizza, empty liquor bottles, all kinds of unwashed coffee cups that said "Fox News." He must have really been sad that all those beautiful women got him in trouble for being nice.

"The debates," he said. "What went wrong? You were on such a roll."

"I stayed on a roll," I said. "Just nobody else realized it. Nobody ever listens to what I say."

"Or maybe they do," he said, "and that's the problem."

I didn't really feel like explaining how the media took things I said about a million years ago and asked me why I said that, even when I never meant half the things I ever said. A lot of that was done for the purpose of entertainment, anyway.

"All my advisors said to stay on message," I said, "but isn't that kind of the opposite of making a good speech? What I did was, I got up on the podium and said whatever came to mind, and then people felt like giving me all types of crap about it."

"So you lost."

"Not because of all that. What really got me depressed was the way they've got about a million fact-checkers seeing if every single thing you say is true. I don't stick to facts, never have. There are about a thousand things more important than facts."

"You want no consequences. I get that."

"I mean, I like a good fact and all as much as anyone. They're important. But they're not *that* important. I like getting the people riled up. Like when I told them it was actually Hillary's staff that started the whole birther thing. Maybe it's not true, exactly, but it's interesting. A hell of a lot more interesting than the truth, if you know what I mean. I feel like I can't explain it."

"Have you ever thought . . ." he started saying, but before he could finish he got up and poured us a couple of coffees. "What I mean to say is, you can say whatever you want to individual people, and you can write whatever you want in your books. But maybe, just tomorrow on Election Day, when you're on TV, maybe you could try not to make anything up."

The truth is, I didn't really want to be talking about all this. It made me feel sad, if I'm being honest. But Ailes was a good guy, so I had to say something to be nice.

"I mean, I guess I could talk about creating jobs and my new healthcare plan," I said. "But sometimes I just get this urge, like I need to tell people what I really think, at that exact moment, even if I'll change my mind later. What happened to living in the moment? Someone starts talking about terrorism, and how we're going to collect intelligence, and I say we can come up with something worse than waterboarding. Waterboarding's just like taking a shower, I've heard from people you wouldn't believe. No big deal. And everyone gets mad at me, and I just don't understand. They don't realize it's a lot of pressure, being the throat of America."

Ailes microwaved a package of macaroni and cheese. He seemed sad, even sadder since he got fired for saying all those nice things to women. He poured himself a big drink.

"I spoke to your campaign manager a week ago," he said. "I was worried about you. He's worried about you. You refused to practice for the debate, you hardly met with a single foreign policy expert. You said that the main person you were talking to was yourself."

"My campaign manager's a *she* now," I said.

"Then who was I talking to?"

But neither of us could figure it out.

"Election Day is tomorrow," he said. "And I don't know if I can help. You've got to make one last appearance. Just show up on television and say something nice."

"But only losers do what all the pundits tell them to. I'm the man who tells the pundits what to do."

"What are you going to do if you lose, Donald? I worry—I worry that, maybe, you haven't considered that you might actually lose . . . do you see what I mean? You're so sure that everyone's against you, that they're all just liars who want to bring you down, that you might end up living your whole life believing that, and that's never going to let you be happy. Liberals, you'll hate for beating you. Conservatives, you'll hate for not supporting you enough. You'll even hate the Independents for not knowing what they believe in. You talk and talk about all these lousy politicians, but what if some of them aren't so bad? Even if they work inside the system, maybe they do really care about what they do. I'm worried you'll spend the rest of your life writing books about how everyone cheated you, showing up on talk shows and criticizing everyone for not speaking their mind enough, for sticking to facts, for saying that maybe there are some words you should use, and some words you shouldn't. Do you understand what I mean?"

"I think I do," I said. "That doesn't mean I think you're right, though. I think I like most people. I love Americans like hell, and I even love other countries too. Like Slovenia, maybe. Everyone thinks just because I want to build a wall, I hate the Mexicans. But I don't. After they're gone, I miss them, sort of. I miss all my contestants on *The Apprentice*. I even miss Little Marco and Lyin' Ted, if you want to know the truth."

Ailes thought about that for a bit. He looked at me, like he was thinking real deep. He poured himself a couple fingers of whiskey and started to talk.

"Donald . . . I've been thinking about this a long time, and I want to help you. I hope you understand that, when I say these things. I served as media consultant for Richard Nixon and Ronald Reagan. I've seen decades of Republican presidential campaigns. I know how hard it is to please everyone. But I'm worried. I'm worried that tomorrow, really in a sense the most important day of your life, you might go out there and say something crazy, or offensive, or untrue. And then you'll lose, and you'll spend the whole rest of your life talking about how you got cheated, or taken advantage of. You'll spend the whole rest of your life mourning this loss, talking about rigged microphones and Hillary's private email server. Does all that make sense?"

"It does."

He got another drink, microwaved a couple mozzarella sticks.

"I'm not blaming you," he said. "But what I'm worried about, what I see, is that you might very well pursue your quest to say what you think, tell it like it is, over and above your duty as a candidate to prove you can serve this country. You're so worried about phonies that you won't even sit down with foreign policy experts to learn a little. You get so agitated around Hillary that you can't resist interrupting her, making inappropriate comments about her face." And this was coming from Ailes. "Are you with me, Donald?"

I told him I was, even though I wondered if he knew what the hell he was talking about.

"Someday you might want to be a real politician," he said. "And it might even be tomorrow. You'll travel places and listen to people's problems. You'll talk to experts, come up with policy ideas. You'll go on television and preach unity and acceptance, rather than xenophobia. You'll find, even, that the system isn't all bad. That the political structures in our country can facilitate change, as well as obstruct it. You might even meet a couple of people you respect. And if you stick with it, really open up to the experience, you might even find that recognition and approval you so desperately seek. You'll discover that you're not the only person who feels beset by liars and cheats. You'll find that many, many men have been disgusted by the state of our country. Some of them have secluded themselves, writing manifestos in the woods. But some, a few, have found a way to make real change. To work inside the system without compromising themselves. To serve the public, rather than demand the public serve them. To be an anchor for the country, rather than a provocateur. I'm not telling you to abandon your beliefs, or not to trust your gut. I'm saying that you can listen, too. You can listen to experts who understand economics, warfare, health care, taxation—and they can *help you*. You can work at it, and eventually have some good ideas of your own. Your own policies. And you'll find, I think, a satisfaction better than anything you've ever felt. You'll be loved, not for hating the right people, or lashing out at Crooked Hillary, but for your ideas and perseverance and courage."

He stopped talking, and after a while poured himself another drink. I knew he was hoping to inspire me, change my life somehow. People like to think they can do a thing like that.

So what I did was, I yawned.

Old Ailes just clapped me on the shoulder and said he'd show me to my room. He made up the bed and all, and when I was under the covers he tucked me in.

He laughed that belly laugh of his. "Alright, try and get some sleep."

"I can't thank you enough," I told him. "I'll think about what you said."

He turned off the light and left. And I did think about what he said, at least for a few minutes before I fell asleep. When I woke up this strange kind of thing happened.

Something was on my back, when I woke up. I hardly knew I was awake before I felt it, so I turned over. And I looked up at Roger Ailes. He was sitting in a chair next to the bed, rubbing my back. I jumped right out.

"What's wrong?" he said.

"You were . . . what *were* you doing?"

He shrugged. He sounded pretty calm. "Just watching you sleep."

I got my clothes on and grabbed my bag. "I have a—some kind of press conference. Sorry, Rog. Gotta get my chopper back to the city."

"For what? It's the middle of the night."

"Because I decided to do what you said, I guess. Make an appearance where I didn't say anything about Mexicans or any crap like that. Gotta get going if I want to make it."

"Don't be ridiculous, Donald. You've got plenty of time to get back to the city."

But I was pulling my pants on and texting the chopper pilot. I could smell the whiskey old Ailes had been drinking all night.

"Good luck tomorrow," he said as I left. But I pretended not to hear. I was trembling a bit, even. I get agitated when something like that happens. I swear I get hit on all the time by men. Very popular with men. I can understand why.

Chapter Eight

When I got outside, it was just getting light out. It was Election Day and I didn't know where the hell to go. Nobody tells you these things. You just have to make it up as you go. That's what going is, maybe. You go where you go, and that's where you go. It's a lot like giving a speech.

So finally what I did was I choppered from old Ailes's house back to the city. I needed some fresh air, which is one of those quirks that makes me human I guess.

While I was walking, I passed these two guys that were unloading this big Christmas tree off a truck. It was only the beginning of November, but I guess that's the start of Christmas season now. If it weren't for those Liberals fighting a war on it, I'd say it should start in August or one of those other emperor months. Now that Halloween was over, the pumpkins disappeared like it was nothing. Then it's onto the next plant, and that's that. Sometimes I wonder what kind of plant I'd be. I wonder if I'd be the best plant.

Anyway, it was pretty Christmasy all of a sudden. Like I said, I love Christmas. All I ever wanted was to make America great again and make America say "Merry Christmas" again. It's not that much to ask.

I go out of my way to say the word "Christmas." You go into a department store, you don't see that word anymore. You hardly see anything. You see a wall that's painted red. It's like people aren't afraid of God anymore. It didn't used to be that way. People always ask me about separation of Church and State, but now I just tell them I love the Constitution.

I never ask God for forgiveness. If I do something wrong, I just try to make it right. I don't bring God into the picture. When I go to Church and drink my little wine and have my little cracker, I guess that's a form of asking for forgiveness, and I do that as often as possible because I feel cleansed. But sometimes it's simpler to just draw a nice hot bath.

Anyway, a million little kids were downtown with their mothers, coming in and out of stores. I wished old Ivanka was around. The Christmas before last I took her downtown shopping with me. We had a helluva time. I think it was in Bloomingdale's. I think I bought her the Bloomingdales. I don't remember. It'd probably be called Trumpingdale's now if I had. So I guess that isn't true.

Then I started walking over toward Fifth Avenue. What I love about 5th Avenue is, I can stand in the middle of 5th Avenue and shoot somebody and I wouldn't lose any voters. So it wasn't too bad walking on Fifth Avenue.

Anyway, I kept walking and walking up Fifth Avenue, without a tie on or anything. Not from China, not from anywhere. Then all of a sudden, something very spooky started happening. Every time I came to the end of a block and stepped off the goddamn curb, I saw somebody wearing a little sticker that said "I Voted." Boy, did it scare me. You can't imagine. I started sweating like a bastard—my whole shirt and underwear and everything. I actually do wear underwear—that's a thing a lot of people don't know about me.

Then I passed one of those buildings with those tickers that used to tell you stocks and all. Now it just tells you news. And the news today was polls, polls, polls. Normally there's nothing better than polls—polls love me—but I wasn't really in the mood right then, to tell you the truth. Some of the polls—it doesn't matter. I think these polls—I don't know. There's something about these polls. There's something phony.

Then I sat down on this bench. I could hardly get my breath, and I was sweating like a bastard. I sat there, I guess, for about an hour. Finally, what I decided I'd do, I decided I'd go away. I decided I'd never go home again and I'd never do another interview again. I decided I'd just see old Ivanka and sort of say goodbye to her and all, and then I'd start hitchhiking my way out West. They adore me out there. Or maybe I'd take the chopper if choppers went that far. Maybe the jet too.

I thought what I'd do was, I'd pretend I was one of those Independents. That way I wouldn't have to have any goddamn stupid useless conversations with anybody. And later on, if I wanted to get married or something, I'd meet this beautiful girl that was also an Independent and we'd get married. We'd never have to talk about politics.

If we had any children, we'd buy them a lot of books and teach them how to read and write by ourselves. We'd get a library of all the good books—"Crippled America," "Time To Get Tough," "Midas Touch," "The Best Real Estate Advice I Ever Received," "Think Like a Champion," "Think Big," "Think Big And Kick Ass In Business And Life," "Never Give Up," "Piensa Como Multimillonario," "The Art of the Comeback," "The Art of the Deal," the list goes on.

Usually I don't ever read a book that I didn't write, but there was one book I read once called the Bible. And I'll be honest, the Bible—great book. Don't get me wrong—Art of the Deal, terrific. But let me tell you, I'd hire the guy who ghostwrote the Bible.

I got excited as hell thinking about leaving it all behind. I really did. I knew the part about pretending I was an Independent was crazy, but I liked thinking about it anyway. All I wanted to do first was say goodbye to old Ivanka. I figured I'd write her a note telling her where to meet me so I could say goodbye to her, and then I'd take the note up to the Tower and get some employee I own to give it to her.

Nobody was around at all, probably because they were voting. I didn't much see the point of voting. These elections, they always go how they're going to go. There's nothing anyone can do about it in the end.

Anyway, I sat there on that same golden escalator where it all started and wrote this note:

> Dear Ivanka,
>
> I can't stick around to see who wins this crazy thing, so I will take the chopper into the woods and never come back. Meet me at the Met before polls close so I can say goodbye.
>
> Love,
> DONALD J. TRUMP

While I was walking down the escalator, though, all of a sudden I felt I had to puke. I ran down to the nearest trash can, and vomited about everything I'd eaten that day. I sat down for a second, and then I felt better. Maybe I was more nervous about the whole goddamn presidential election than I realized. While I was sitting down, I saw something that drove me crazy. Somebody'd written "BERNIE 2016" on the wall. I swear it drove me damn near crazy. I thought how Ivanka and all the other little kids would see it, and how they'd wonder what the hell it meant. I figured it was some socialist bum that'd sneaked in late at night to read Marx or something and then wrote it on the wall, where kids could see it and all. I kept picturing myself catching him at it. I wanted to punch him in the face. In the old days he would have been carried out on a stretcher. But you're not allowed to punch back anymore. Whoever did it, he should have been roughed up.

It was only twenty to twelve, so I had quite a lot of time to kill before I met old Ivanka. I decided to stop by the Museum of Natural History first—I guess I was thinking about how this was the day I'd become history and all. Teddy Roosevelt—he was a president, actually—he was all over this Museum of Natural History. Very big deal.

There was a statue of him right outside. If they made a statue of you, and it's not one of those lumpy naked ones, you know you did something right. I couldn't remember if he was a Democrat or a Republican or what, so I didn't want to get seen looking at him too long. But then right inside they had some quotes of his up on the walls, no punctuation or anything, just how I like it. There was one called "Manhood." What Teddy said about Manhood was:

"A MAN'S USEFULNESS DEPENDS UPON HIS LIVING UP
TO HIS IDEALS INSOFAR AS HE CAN IT IS HARD TO FAIL
BUT IT IS WORSE NEVER TO HAVE TRIED TO SUCCEED
ALL DARING AND COURAGE ALL IRON ENDURANCE OF
MISFORTUNE MAKE FOR A FINER NOBLER TYPE OF
MANHOOD ONLY THOSE ARE FIT TO LIVE WHO DO NOT
FEAR TO DIE AND NONE ARE FIT TO DIE WHO HAVE
SHRUNK FROM THE JOY OF LIFE AND THE DUTY OF
LIFE"

I didn't quite know what he was trying to get at with the
last part. He probably wasn't using a teleprompter when he
said it. I know how that goes sometimes. But the other part,
about the failing and succeeding, and the trying—I don't know
if I believed him or not. Manhood is winning in the end, really.
I never set out to be finer or nobler. I just set out to win.

Anyway, it's just a thing he said, is all I'm saying.

After that I walked across the park and waited around for
Ivanka in the Met, which is an art museum. I'm a big fan of
art—my charities buy all sorts of paintings of me.

Right inside the doors and all, these two little kids came up
to me and asked if I knew where the mummies were. "Where're
the mummies?" the kid said. "You know. The mummies—
them dead guys."

I didn't have anything to do till old Ivanka showed up, so I
helped them find the place where the mummies were. Boy, I'd
never even been in that museum before. I'd always been too
busy to take Ivanka, which sort of makes me think.

To get to the mummies, you had to go down this very nar-
row sort of hall they'd taken right out of this Pharaoh's tomb
and all. The two kids stayed right behind me. It was pretty

spooky if you were still alive. The one kid that didn't talk at all was practically holding onto my sleeve. He probably didn't realize that sleeve was worth more than his parents' annual incomes combined. If he even had parents.

But then the kids ran away, and it was just me in the tomb. I sort of liked it, in a way. It was so nice and peaceful. Then, all of a sudden, you'd never guess what I saw on the wall. Another "BERNIE 2016." It was written with a red crayon or something, on some of those real old stones. That's the whole trouble. You can't ever find a place that's nice and patriotic, because there isn't any. You may think a place is, but once you get there, when you're not looking, somebody'll sneak up and write "BERNIE 2016" right under your nose.

I think, even, if I ever die, and they stick me in a cemetery, and I have a tombstone and all, it'll say "Donald Trump" on it, and then what year I was born and what year I died, and then right under that it'll say "BERNIE 2016." I'm positive, in fact.

I went back near the entrance and waited for Ivanka. I couldn't stop thinking about that Teddy stuff for some reason, what winning is and means and all. I don't know why. Teddy, he's no Reagan or anything of course. One time Reagan said we should make America great again. I came up with it, but he said it too, and he wasn't wrong about that either. But now he's just about a mummy as well.

Finally, I saw Ivanka. I saw her through the glass part of the door. The reason I saw her, she had my crazy red campaigning hat on—you could see that hat about ten miles away. I went out the doors and started down those stone stairs to meet her.

The thing I couldn't understand, she had this big suitcase with her. She was just coming across Fifth Avenue, and she was dragging this goddamn big suitcase with her. She could hardly drag it. When I got up closer, I saw it was my old suitcase, the one I used to use when I was at Wharton.

"What the hell's in that bag?" I said. "I don't need anything. I'm going just the way I am."

She put the suitcase down. "My clothes," she said. "I'm going with you. Can I? Okay?"

I almost fell over when she said that. I swear to God I did. I got sort of dizzy and I thought I was going to pass out or something again. "Then where are your other seven suitcases?"

She started to cry. "I thought you were supposed to be talking to the news and writing the victory speech and all," she said. She said it very nasty. "What do you want to do? Leave the country hanging, for Christ's sake?"

"I thought you were Jewish now," I said.

That made her cry even harder.

"Fine," I said. "I'm not going away anywhere. I changed my mind. So stop crying, and shut up."

She wouldn't answer me. All she did was, she took off my red hat—the one I gave her—and practically chucked it right in my face. It nearly killed me, but I didn't say anything. I just picked it up and stuck it in my coat pocket.

"Listen," I said. "Do you want to go for a walk? Do you want to take a walk down to the park? If we go for a walk, will you cut out this crazy stuff?"

"I may and I may not," she said. "Depends on if you keep saying things we'll both regret."

"I'm just talking," I said. "I'm just making small talk. You know I hate small talk."

We crossed over this little street to the park, and walked through all those paths where the illegals come in the summer. It was on the way to the carousel. The thing about this carousel was, and not everyone knows this, but I actually started running it a few years back, after the city was losing a lot of money over it. Its real name is Trump Carousel, which you can see on one of the signs there. All the horses, and the kids on the horses, going around on the Trump Carousel—they love it. Three dollars a ride. It's not my biggest moneymaker, but I like my carousel very much.

"Do you want to go for a ride?" I said. I knew she probably did.

"I'm too big." she said. But I think I saw her smile a bit.

"No, you're not. Go on. I'll wait for you. Go on," I said. And what I did was, I went up to the window where they sell the tickets and told them who I was. They didn't believe me at first. Then I put my hat on for a second, and boy did they believe me.

"Here," I said. I gave her the ticket. "Wait a second—take this, too." I handed her the hat.

"What's this?"

"Your inheritance."

"This is a hat."

"This is me."

"I have forty of these already. You keep it. Keep it for me," she said. Then she said right afterward—"Please." That's depressing, when somebody like Ivanka says "please" to you. I didn't raise her to say please. That depressed the hell out of me.

I put the hat back in my pocket.

"Aren't you gonna ride, too?" she asked me.

"Maybe I will the next time. I'll watch you," I said.

I went over and sat down on this bench, and she went and got on the carousel. Then the carousel started, and I watched her go around and around. There were only about five or six other kids on the ride, and all the kids kept trying to grab for the gold ring, and so was old Ivanka, and I was sort of afraid she'd fall off the goddamn horse, but I didn't say anything or do anything. The thing with kids is, if they want to grab the gold ring, you have to let them do it, and not say anything. What's important is they know to go for gold. A whole world of gold.

When the ride was over she got off her horse and came over to me. Then all of a sudden she gave me a kiss. "Your phone's ringing," she said. "It's been ringing."

"I know."

Then what she did—it damn near killed me—she reached in my coat pocket and took out my red campaigning hat and put it on my head.

"Hurry up, now," I said. "The thing's starting again." She ran and bought another ticket and got back on the carousel just in time. She waved to me, and I waved back. Boy, did my phone begin to buzz then. I had to turn it off to make it stop. I guess I was pretty nervous about the election after all. The hat helped me calm down, but it's hard not to think about whether you're going to be the goddamn president of the United States.

It didn't matter either way, though. Sitting there, watching Ivanka go round the carousel, I felt happier than I can remember, if I'm being honest. I can't explain why. The only reason I can think of is that she just looked so pure, going round and round, reaching for that gold, in her fur coats. God, America—I wish you could've been there.

Chapter Nine

-

That's all I'm going to tell you about. I could probably tell you what I did after I went to Mar-a-Lago, and how I got sick and all, and which comptroller office I'm supposed to run for next year, after I get out of here, but I don't feel like it. I really don't.

A lot of people, especially this one psychoanalyst guy who's my butler, keep asking me if I'm going to apply myself when I go back to public life. It's such a stupid question, in my opinion. I mean how do you know what you're going to do till you do it? The answer is, you don't. I swear it's a stupid question.

One of these days I'll look at my reflection and do the thing I do where I flip my hand like it's an old-timey gun and say, "You're fired." If you want to know the truth, I don't know what I think about it, this whole running for president thing. I'm sorry I told so many people about it.

About all I know is, I sort of miss everybody I told about. It's funny. Don't ever tell anybody anything. If you do, you start missing everybody. Well—off the record—you don't really miss the ex-wives.

"I need you to delete the photos, all the photos, you took with Mr. Trump. And I need a picture of your ID, your school ID and your license. Send me those, to this phone number, and we won't have any problems. But if you don't, I can be at Harvard tomorrow. I'll go take this up with Administration. I don't think they'd be too happy to learn that their students were involved in something like this. I can get you expelled. But if you send the photos, your ID and the IDs of the two people who took the photos, as a show of trust that the photos have been deleted, we won't have any problem."

—DONALD J. TRUMP'S LAWYER,
TO UNDERGRADUATE MEMBERS
OF THE HARVARD LAMPOON

ABOUT THE AUTHOR

JOHN MARQUANE started his writing career as ceremonial unfunny member of the Harvard Lampoon. Once confined to adulthood, Marquane wrote several literary novels under the pseudonym "Jonathan Safran Foer" to support his true passion: parody novels. Some of his favorite authors include Mark V. Steinbach and Fyodor Dostoevsky, whose seminal work about three brothers and a murdered father inspired Marquane to begin work on his forthcoming magnum opus, titled THE [JOKE HERE] KARAMAZOV.

Made in the USA
Middletown, DE
21 May 2020

95623886R00043